Copyright © 2023 by Morwer.

Cover image: *Monochrome Dark Woman Photo Book Cover* by pixel_aesthetic.

Designed on Canva.

All rights reserved.

No part of this work may be used or reproduced in any manner whatsoever, without written permission of the author, except for brief quotations used for promotion or in reviews. This is a work of fiction.

Section 17

by

Morwenna Blackwood

Also by the author:

The (D)Evolution of Us

Glasshouse

Underrated

Skin and Bone

(Bestselling noir thriller novels, published by #darkstrokebooks.)

Section 17

is a collection of poetry inspired by my struggles with mental illness. I was diagnosed with Obsessive Compulsive Order and Depression when I was fourteen. Some of these poems were written as part of my MA Creative Writing course eight years ago; and amidst the chaos in the world – micro- and macrocosmic – I have added to them and decided to publish them now.

Let me know what you make of them, at www.morwennablackwoodauthor.com.

Free Will

I was the only one.

I was the only one allowed out.

I wasn't allowed out by myself.

And I had to come back.

No, I had to be *brought* back.

But I had to be *willing* to come back.

If I wasn't willing to come back,

I wouldn't be allowed out again –

Ironically, it was threatening to call me a

'Voluntary' patient.

In fact, it I hadn't complied in the first place, I wouldn't have been

'Voluntary' (which sounds redundant, but it's really important).

If I hadn't said 'yes, I'll come in',

I wouldn't have been allowed out. I'd have been

Sectioned (with a capital 's')

And it would have been a question of

Numbers, not words.

Charcoal

I told them I would be off work next week.

I stared at my hand, screwed up tight in my lap.

The ambulance lady lay her hand on

My shoulder, saying it would be alright.

She asked me to drink a mix of charcoal

In cold water, in a white plastic cup.

I told her it was crunchy, and she laughed.

A few tiny pieces floated on top

But most of it lurked under the water;

Staining it black from the bottom upwards,

Polluting clean water with ebony –

The antidote for my poisoned body.

I wondered if my mouth would go black.

I'd made the attempt; I couldn't go back.

(Self-)Harm

That morning –

The last time we saw each other –

You came up with

Enough Marmite on toast for

Everyone but me.

Me: three gashes and

Still bleeding through the paper towel,

A whopping hangover and

No one would speak to me.

No one even asked if I was okay.

You said, 'Are you still here?'

I didn't get it. Any of it.

And I didn't understand you.

So I left.

High

and a wise man once wrote:

What is man but a mass of thawing clay?

and on mornings like these, bodies melt to arms,

arms to hands to fingers to short nails

painted azure like the sky. I am ecstatic; I breathe

 a sigh on the wind, whizzing in a blue car

to the beach. Devon is bathing in yellow,

buttercups and birds, myriad words whispered on the rush

of waves; ssh, ssh, listen to the gulls and the chaffinches …

in trees to branches to leaves to blossom

to fruits … taste the sunshine,

that effuses light to life to the wise man who once wrote:

Earth laughs in flowers

and it does - look at the roses, busy with bees,

and the bumbling flight of the butterfly,

on this high hill here with dandelions,

daisies and grass i stretch out on,

melting like a mass of thawing clay,

the day eternal,

and the rest of my life, my creation

the cosmos and the core of the earth,

a mass of clay, laughing in flowers …

which open like the sun and fade like the day

to stars, daisies in the sky, yellow, green and blue,

in the morning i walk on the grass in the dew

and feel desire, spreading like a melting lolly,

i hug the hedge like the sparkling spiders' webs

like so many layers, glued with love

on this canvas of … the one above …?

for what is anything but the need to know,

 to fly like a gull to the beach to the sand

that was hills, with lush green grass on

green blood. i wash myself into the world this day

like a mass of thawing clay

(Quotes from: Henry David Thoreau's *Spring;* and Ralph Waldo Emerson's *Hamatreya.*)

Into the Sea

I'm throwing the necklace into the sea.

I remember when he bought it for me:

When I got my 'A' level results we

Went out to celebrate, out for tea and

There it was: silver – not silver-plated –

Thick and heavy like a snake waiting for

Me on the black velvet in the black case,

And I wore it when he came to see me,

Drinking tea in a café by the sea.

Then, and only then. It was so heavy.

Then, one day, he stopped coming, and now I'm

Here, throwing the necklace into the sea.

Soap

The end has come.

I knew it would; something had to happen

One day. They went shopping

And didn't replace the soap.

No soap.

How am I supposed to clean

The house without soap?

How do I rinse off the chemicals

Of the cleaning products

Without soap? How do I wash

The poisons and the germs

Off my hands? Off the tiles

And the floor where they've splashed?

I am Popeye

Without his spinach.

I am Batman

Without the Bat Cave.

I am Clarke Kent

Without a conveniently-placed phone box.

Don't they realise I'm

Keeping them safe?!

There's no soap.

I'm trying to keep them safe

And they went shopping

And didn't replace the soap.

This is the end.

Low

And Brecht once wrote:

Killing oneself / Is a slight affair

And the act may be, but we are inextricably linked

And it won't just be about

Me on that dark day of

Freezing wind and rain like tears

Hurling themselves onto the windscreen

Of the funeral car as they crawl

To the cold cemetery with cold hands;

Icy hearts splintering while

Rooks are blown across the sky, and from above

The chapel door a raven watches them;

And I feel like Seamus Heaney who once wrote:

How did I end up like this?

A mother buying lilies for her daughter to place on

The coffin, lilies and hellebores, petals

Quickly sodden; wondering if it's true,

What Larkin wrote: *They fuck you up, your mum and dad.*

I know it wasn't their fault, my moods

Like the sea, exquisite and dreadful,

My creations complex as the cosmos. I write

That I wonder how I ended up like this,

So infinitely, straighjacketedly sad;

Maybe it'll be a slight affair to me,

Just another day,

Just slightly deeper cuts on my arms tonight

Which bleed through grey to blue to

Dawn, and the mess, and the smell;

How did we end up like this?

The lot of us separate as stanzas,

Whole as a poem, just another

Group of people in black

Crying down to the earth, as

Slight an affair as a

Rainy Wednesday, as

Trudging through the supermarket

For bread and milk.

We end up feeding the land we fed off,

And it's exquisite and dreadful.

(Quotes from: Bertoit Brecht, *Epistle on Suicide;* Seamus Heaney, *Exposure;* Philip Larkin, *This Be the Verse.*)

The Gulls

Perched on the bench outside the hospital.

The sunshine comforting upon my legs,

A flock of seagulls play beyond the roof;

They dive and fight; I'm sure they're having fun,

While I sit here and wonder what life means,

And open up another box of pills.

And open yet another box of pills.

I have a meeting at the hospital,

To see if I can walk with my own legs,

Figuratively speaking; it's not fun

To sit and talk and wonder what life means.

I still feel that I could jump off the roof.

I really want to jump right off the roof

And land upon my head and not my legs.

At thirty I've still not had any fun,

I've spent a lot of time in hospital,

And I've been on so many bloody pills

And sat and talked and wondered what life means.

We sit and ponder what my life should mean

And up the dose and try me on more pills.

Meanwhile I battle with my thoughts – what fun(!)

And sit here with the sunshine on my legs

And watch the young gulls crying on the roof.

I cry and cry outside the hospital.

Ironic I should be at hospital,

Sat here while gulls wheel around the roof.

I want to go and join them and have fun,

Not sit here, dying, swallowing these pills;

Coz I don't have a clue what my life means.

Imbibing meds. The sun shines on my legs.

I can't stand up. I'm wobbly on my legs.

They find me a place at a psych hospital.

An ambulance comes, god, what does this mean?

The gulls are blurry and so is the roof.

They confiscate my wine and all my pills

And get me to drink charcoal – it's not fun.

So now I sit and wonder what life means.

The doors are locked, there's mesh on the roof,

And plastic cups – no birds – and lots more pills.

Don't Tell

Don't tell

Coz no one cares.

They wouldn't believe you,

Anyway. They'd just call you a

Liar.

Homemade

Next to the square window

By the round table

Stood his chair.

It was high and hard, with a straight back

In a paisley pattern;

Grey and green and blue.

It stood empty

In the homely room.

He made a me matchstick boat

From that chair, spending days

Gluing matchstick after matchstick

Together to make a boat that

Would never float.

He made me a doll's house

From that chair, spending days

Expertly gluing on the sides and the stairs

But I didn't have any dolls,

Just stuffed animals.

In that chair, I sat on his lap

In a new green skirt, aged twelve.

Now that chair stood empty

And I was glad.

I prayed that nobody would ever sit in it again.

Cousins

He gave me a rose the day I turned ten,

I remembered when the flashbacks began.

Visions of all that had happened back when

We were children, and inseparable, and

We spent the holidays at Grandma's house.

We made dens, and that's where he caught me once –

Out of sight of the house, of Grandma, out of

Sight of our parents – they were having lunch –

And were calling us to come quickly.

That time I was playing on the swing …

Why me? Why did he have to pick me?

He made up for it by giving me things.

When I sat on his lap in that green skirt

Childhood was over and I felt like dirt.

Have I Been Sectioned?

I am stuck with OCD –

I cannot leave the house –

What I wouldn't give to be free.

The tiles are dirty – Look! See?!

I disinfect the house.

I am stuck with OCD.

There are germs all over me –

I douse myself with soap – I douse and douse –

What I wouldn't give to be free.

I can't use coins or notes anymore.

I'll never have a spouse.

I am stuck with OCD.

In hospital I stay four weeks –

I can't get off the couch –

What I wouldn't give to be free.

These drugs, they make me so sleepy

And quiet as a mouse.

What I wouldn't give to be free – but

I am stuck with OCD.

(H)Ours

We tell the time by when our pills come, in their little plastic shot glasses, sitting on a chair in the meds room (they come and get you).

Mornings I have one and a half,

Evenings I have five.

Both times with half a plastic tumbler of water poured from that looming plastic jug. If I get up during the day, or during the night, to be part of the stretched long straightjacket hours of boredom, I get one or two more, little white Tick Tacks of solace. I stare at the wall, waiting for dawn, waiting for dusk, waiting to be saved; watching the shadows shortening or lengthening, watching the seasons change; I imagine a minute hand struggling around a clock face. I wear my quilt like it's a force field, like I'm frigid, stuck here like a bug in amber. Have I been here forever? Will I be here forever? We tell the time by when our pills come -

One and a half and it's morning,

Five and it's night.

I'm Telling

I told,

In a letter,

What they needed to know;

And CBT wasn't enough,

I wrote.

Compliance

Compliance comes from

Fear and despair.

Compliance is a shutting down.

'If you choose this, things will be

Better.'

'Better, for whom?'

Being a *good girl* – being

Compliant –

Got me into this mess in the first place.

And there was no choice, by the way.

If it had been in the olden days,

It would have been me

Lighting the gas.

Stimming

Is this what they mean by the

First sign of madness?

I write the car number plate in the air when I'm stressed.

(They call it 'triggered' now.)

And it turns out I don't have a

Weird kind of Tourette's,

Even though I sometimes

Spontaneously whisper stuff I don't mean.

This is boring. You get the picture.

But I can't stop.

Yep, it's probably the

First sign of madness.

Getting On With It

I don't think there is such a thing as

The Meaning Of Life.

I think it's a case of

Just getting on with it.

In spite of my heart-felt attempts, things just

Happen.

Chaos, with or without the theory.

So I'll take the pills,

Now I've sampled all the therapies;

Now I – and I quote – know them better than

The professionals professing them.

I'll take the pills

For the rest of my life,

Whether I'm a slave to Big Pharma;

Whether 'they' are asserting some kind of

Control over me;

Whether or not it's psychosomatic.

I'll take the pills

Despite the stigma and the discrimination and

The minds made up at first glance.

I'll take the pills

Because I'm better than I've ever been.

I'll take the pills because

They help me

Get on with it.

(Also, I think there's a good chance I'm addicted.)

About the author

When she was six years old, Morwenna wrote an endless story about a frog, and hasn't stopped writing since. She has an MA in Creative Writing, and can usually be found down by the sea. She often thinks about that frog.

Milton Keynes UK
Ingram Content Group UK Ltd.
UKHW052015310723
426074UK00025B/1301